WHEN THE BURDS FLY FREE;

A Guide to Compassionate Boundaries and Emotional Freedom

Written By

Laura K McLeod

TABLE OF CONTENTS

Contents

INTRODUCTION:

THE WEIGHT OF YES

Picture this: You're walking through the quiet woods, the kind where sunlight spots the path and leaves rustle like old friends. Your steps feel easy at first, full of that good warmth from lending a hand to a neighbor, a coworker, maybe even a stranger who needed a kind word. It's simple, right? Helping feels like the right thing. It connects you, makes your heart hum a little louder.

But then, bit by bit, something shifts. Those small yeses start to add up. A quick favor here, an extra listen there. At first, you don't notice the change. It's soft, like a feather landing on your shoulder. But soon, there are more clinging to your back, your arms, your thoughts. They don't weigh much alone. Together? They slow you down. Your steps drag. The woods feel thicker, the light a little dimmer. You keep going because stopping means letting someone down. And who wants that?

If this sounds familiar, you're in good company. Hi, I'm here with you. This book is for the quiet helpers, the ones who say yes even when their tank is low, who spot a need before it's spoken, who give because it's woven into who they are. Maybe you're a parent always on call, a friend everyone leans on, or someone at work who picks up the slack without a word. You love deeply, and that's your strength. But lately, that love has started to feel heavy. Tired. Like you're carrying a flock of little burden burds, if you will, that weren't meant to stay.

You might have picked this up because of Barnaby and the Burds, that short story about a kind rabbit who learns this the hard way. Barnaby hops through his forest, helping everyone, until the burds (those standing for all we take on) cover him so thick he can't move. It's a simple tale, but it hits home because we've all been there, bent low under yeses that promised connection but stole our breath. If you haven't read it yet, no worries; it's not required. But if you have, you know that ache when Barnaby finally sits still, tears falling, and hears a wise voice say: A no can be kind too.

That's the heart of this guide. When the Burds Fly Free isn't about becoming less caring. It's about the Loving

No Method, a simple way to say no that keeps your heart open, without guilt or walls. It's for when you want to help but need to choose yourself first. Because here's the truth: Boundaries aren't selfish. They're the ground that lets your kindness grow strong and true. When you practice this, those burds lift off. Your steps lighten. You show up better for others and yourself.

We'll walk it together, step by quiet step. No big leaps, just small shifts that add up. By the end, you'll have tools to spot your burds, words to set them free, and a new feel for yes that comes from rest, not rush. You're not alone in these woods. Let's find the path to peace.

Think about last week. How many times did you say yes when a small voice inside whispered wait? Maybe it was staying late for a team that's not yours, or biting back no to a family plan that drained you dry. Or that friend who calls at midnight, and you listen even as your eyes burn. These aren't bad things; they're signs of your big heart. But when yes becomes a habit, it costs. Energy fades. Joy hides. Connections strain, because giving from empty leaves little real warmth.

I see this all the time in the people I coach, folks just like you, full of care but running low. Take Sarah, a teacher who planned every class party, every parent teacher meet, until weekends blurred into work. She thought it made her good at her job. Until one day, she snapped at a kid over nothing, tears hot on her face after. Or Mike, a dad who fixed everyone's car, mowed every lawn, until his own kids asked why he never played ball anymore. These stories aren't rare. They're the quiet pull of people-pleasing: We help to feel needed, but it flips. We end up lost in the load.

The good news? You can change it. The Loving No Method starts right here, with one breath. Try this now, it's your first tool, called the Burd Pause. Sit where you are. Close your eyes if it helps. Breathe in slowly for four counts: Feel your feet on the ground, like roots in soft earth. Hold for four: Notice any tightness, any yes that sticks. Breathe out for six: Let one small weight go, like a feather on wind. Say to yourself: "I get to choose." Open your eyes. How's that feel? A bit lighter? That's the start.

(Chapter 1), what they cost if you carry them too long.

(Chapter 2), And what a Loving No really means

(Chapter 3). Then, the how: Three pillars to make it real (Chapter 4), practice steps and words you can use today (Chapter 5), and how it leads to yeses that light you up (Chapter 6). Each chapter has a quick reflection—short

You're here because something in you knows: You deserve ease. Kindness that flows both ways. A life where helping feels good again, not gone. Barnaby found it when he learned to hop free, paws light, fur shining. You can too. Let's go. Your first Loving No is waiting, and it's kinder than you think.

Start Here Reflection: What's one yes from this week that felt heavy? Jot it down. We'll come back to it soon.

CHAPTER 1:

THE ANATOMY OF A BURD

Let's start at the beginning, shall we? With why those little burds show up in the first place. You know the ones I mean, the small, soft weights that land on your shoulder after a yes you weren't sure about. They're not mean or heavy on their own. They're just there, like a friend's quick ask or a work email that needs "just one more thing." But over time, they stick around, and before you know it, you're hopping like Barnaby, carrying a whole flock without even noticing how it started.

In Barnaby and the Burds, that kind rabbit doesn't see the burds coming at first. He says yes to helping a neighbor carry a basket, then yes to listening to a worry, and poof, another burd flutters down. It's innocent. Helping feels good, right? Warm, like sunlight on your fur. But those yeses add up because of something deep inside us: the way we're built to connect, to care, to fit in. And that's okay. It's what makes us human, or in Barnaby's case, rabbit. The trouble comes when we don't see the pattern. When yes becomes the only answer we know.

So, what's the anatomy of a burd? Let's break it down simply, like looking at a leaf under a stream. First, there's the root: fear of letting people down. Think about it. From the time we're small, we're taught that good people help. Say no, and you might hurt a feeling. Or worse, get left out. I hear this from so many folks I coach, a quiet worry that no means you're not nice anymore. Like if you skip that family dinner, they'll think you don't care. Or if you pass on the extra shift, your boss will see you as lazy. It's not true, of course. But that fear whispers loud, and burds love a good whisper.

Take Lisa, a mom I know who coaches soccer on weekends. She started saying yes to every snack run, every uniform wash, every last-minute carpool. Why? "If I don't, the team falls apart. The other parents will judge me." Sound familiar? That fear keeps the yes coming, even when her own kids are asking for a game night at home. One burden after another, until she's shuffling instead of running, just like Barnaby under his growing load.

Then there's the habit part, the old ways we fall into without thinking. We've done it for so long; yes, it feels automatic. Like muscle memory. You get a text: "Can you watch the dog?" Boom, yes, before your brain catches up. It's comfy, in a way. Saying yes keeps things smooth. No awkward talks, no explaining. But habits like that? They sneak burds in the back door. Barnaby didn't question his first burd because helping was his go-to move. "Of course I can," he'd say with that rabbit smile. We do the same. A coworker asks for notes from the meeting she missed. Sure, even if you're buried in your own work. A friend needs to vent about her day? Always, even if yours was rough too.

And don't get me started on the worst piece, the quiet belief that our value is tied to how much we give. This one's sneaky. It says, "If you're not helping, what are you?" Ouch. For caregivers, empaths, and anyone who's wired to tune into others' needs, this hits hard. We feel seen when we're useful, needed when we're there. So, we pile on yeses to prove it. Remember Mike from the intro? The dad fixing cars and mowing lawns? He told me once, "If I'm not doing for them, who am I?" His burds weren't just tasks; they were proof he mattered.

Until they piled so high, he couldn't see his own reflection.

These roots, fear, habit, and worth, aren't flaws. They're human. They come from wanting to belong, to love well. But when we ignore them, burds multiply. One yes feels light. Ten? You're bent low, paws shaking, like Barnaby on that forest floor. The good news is that seeing the anatomy is the first step to change. Once you spot a burd forming, you can choose. Pause. Let it fly off before it sticks.

Why does this matter now? Because carrying too many burds doesn't just tire you out, it dims your light. That warmth from helping? It fades when yes comes from empty. Connections get wobbly because you're giving from a place that's running low. And deep down, you know it. That's why you're here. To understand the why, so the how feels easier.

Let's pause for a second. Take a breath with me. In through your nose, out through your mouth. Feel your feet on the ground. That's your anchor, no burd can pull you from it. Ready to name yours? We'll get to tools soon. But first, a bit more on how these roots grow.

Fear of letting down often starts young. Maybe a parent praised you for being the "easy one," the helper. Or school taught you that fitting in meant going along. Fast-forward, and its baked in. A study I read, a simple one from folks who study feelings, says most of us avoid no because it spikes that "uh-oh" in our gut. Like our brain thinks rejection is around the corner. But here's the shift: Most people aren't waiting to judge. They just want a connection, same as you. Lisa, that soccer mom? When she started picking one or two things to say yes to, the team didn't fall apart. Parents stepped up. And she felt lighter, not less.

Habits are easier to spot once you look. They're the autopilot yeses. Like scrolling your phone and answering every ping. Or saying yes in emails because "maybe later" feels rude. Barnaby's habit was hopping to help without a pause. He didn't see the burds till they covered his eyes. We can do better. Notice the pattern: What asks always get a quick yes from you? Texts from family? Work chats? Spot it, and you can slow down.

The worth tie-in? That's the deepest root. It whispers that you're only good if you're giving. But think of Barnaby after his burds lift, he's still kind. Still hopes to help when it fits. His worth wasn't in the carrying; it was in being himself. Same for you. You're valuable just sitting still, breathing. No, yes required.

Seeing this anatomy isn't about blame. It's about kindness to yourself. Those roots grew for good reasons to protect, to connect. Now, we can tend them differently. Water those that serve, trim those that weigh.

Alright, enough on the "why" for a minute. Let's move to the how, because understanding burds is one thing; spotting them in your day is what sets you free. This is where the Loving No Method starts: With clear eyes on what's landing. We'll use a simple tool called the Spot Your Burds List. It's quick, like jotting a grocery note. No fancy journal needed, just a piece of paper, your phone, or even the back of an envelope.

Here's how it works. Set aside five minutes, maybe tonight before bed, or tomorrow over coffee. Draw three columns: "The Ask," "My Yes," "The Burd." I'll walk you through it quickly, like we're jotting it on a napkin over coffee. This is for Lisa, the soccer mom from earlier—remember her, always baking cookies for the team and driving carpools till her tank ran dry? She's filling out her list after a busy week, naming three recent asks to see the patterns pop.

Here's how her table might look (grab a pen and try your own version—keep it messy; it's for you, not show):

The Ask	**My Yes**	**The Burd (Weight Added)**
Bake cookies for the team's snack tomorrow	"Sure, I'll whip them up tonight."	Less sleep + guilt if I say no (fear root—worried about looking like a bad parent)
Cover the carpool for two families after practice	"No problem, happy to help out."	Skipped my evening walk + resentment building (habit root—auto-yes without checking my energy)
Stay late to chat with Another parent about her kid's drama	"Of course, let's talk it through."	Drained my last bit of patience for my own family dinner (Worth root—feels like it proves I'm the “good" one)

See how it works? The asks are straight from life—no judgment. "My Yes" shows the old pattern (what she said or would say). "The Burd" names the real tug—not just the task, but the root from Chapter 1 and how it adds up to those costs we unpacked in Chapter 2. For Lisa, glancing at this sparked her first Loving No: "I love supporting the team, but baking's not my night—anyone sharing the load?" One burd lighter, her hop a bit bouncier.

Your turn—what's one thing you ask from your week? Jot it in those columns, and watch what lifts. Feels good, right? What's showing up for you?

Do this for three, no more. Why three? Enough to see a pattern, not so much that it overwhelms. When you're done, look back. What's common? Family asks, hitting the fear root? Work one, the habit? Seeing it on paper makes burds less sneaky. Like Barnaby pausing under the oak, first burd lands, and he notices. You can too.

I saw this tool click for Mike, the dad with the lawns. He listed: Ask, "Neighbor's mower broke, can I fix it?" Yes, "Yeah, come over." Burd, "Missed my kid's game (habit, pulls from family time)." After a week of listening, he said, "I see it now. These aren't just favors, they're stealing my yes for what matters." He started picking one burd a day to question. Not all at once. Small hops.

This list isn't a to-do list to fix everything. It's a mirror. It shows your burds without shame. And shame? That's what keeps them stuck. Be gentle, like Sage the tortoise with Barnaby, just sit with it. "You've carried a lot," Sage says. Same as you.

Now, let's dig a touch deeper into each root, because knowing them helps you unhook. Start with fear. It's the burd that chirps loudest: "What if they don't like me?" Or "What if I look selfish?" This comes from our wiring; we're social creatures. Back in cave days, being left out meant danger. Today? It’s unanswered emails, or missed invites. But most no’s

land is softer than we think. A friend might say, "Okay, next time." Boss? "Got it, thanks for letting me know." Practice naming the fear: "I'm scared of disappointing her." Say it out loud. It loses power. Then ask: "What's the real risk?" Often, it's small. Lisa tried it, said no to one carpool. The other mom found a ride. No drama.

Just relief.

Habits are the easy root to shift because they're patterns, not feelings. Track your triggers. Mornings? Afternoons? Certain people? Barnaby's trigger was any animal in need, bam, yes. Yours might be texts (always answer) or meetings (volunteer first). Break it with a pause. Before, yes, count to three. Ask: "Does this fit my day?" Or "What do I need right now?" It's like a speed bump for burds. Mike set his phone to buzz once, not ping nonstop. Gave him space to choose. One week in, fewer auto-yes. More room to breathe.

The worth root takes tenderness. It says your okay-ness depends on output. But flip it: What if your worth is just being? Breathing? Here for the hard days? Barnaby shines brightest after release, not from more helping, but from rest. Try this add-on to your list: After each burd, write one "just because" yes. "Yes, to my tea break." "Yes, to calling a friend for me." Builds the muscle that you matter, not from the pile.

These roots overlap, of course. A work yes might mix fear (boss mad) and worth (prove I'm a team player). That's normal. The Spot Your Burds List catches them all. Do it weekly, Sunday nights work well. Over time, you'll spot burds before they land. Say, "Not today," soft as Barnaby's first no. And watch, as one lifts.

Why keep going? Because this chapter's gift is clarity. You see the anatomy, you name the parts, and suddenly burds aren't mysteries. They're choices. And choices? They lead to lighter steps. Less overwhelm. More you.

One last thing before we move on: This isn't about never saying yes. Barnaby still helps after, when it fits. We're building that too. For now, celebrate spotting. That's huge.

Chapter Reflection: What's one yes from last week that felt off? Write it down. What root fed that burd, fear, habit, worth? No fix yet, just notice. We'll use it next chapter.

CHAPTER 2:

THE COST OF CARRYING

We've spent time in Chapter 1 exploring the origins of those burds, how they flutter into our lives through the fertile soil of fear (that worry of disappointing someone), habit (the automatic yes that skips any second thought), and the deep-seated need to feel our worth tied to how much we can offer others. It's a valuable map, this understanding of where the weight begins, like noticing the first few twigs being woven into a nest before it becomes too sturdy to dismantle easily. But maps only get you so far; they show the terrain, but they don't carry the load for you. To truly step into lighter living, we have to confront what happens when those burds don't just visit but decide to stay: the profound, often subtle cost of carrying them day after day, yes after yes, without a moment's release. This chapter isn't here to shame your generous heart or convince you to stop helping altogether, far from it. It's a compassionate invitation to illuminate the toll, the quiet erosions that can turn a helper's glow into a shuffle, so you can recognize the signs early and choose a path of balance before the flock grows too heavy, echoing Barnaby's own journey through his beloved but burdening woods.

Let's return to Barnaby's tale for a grounding moment, because its simplicity holds such profound truth for us all. That kind-hearted rabbit, with his impossibly soft white fur that caught the dappled sunlight like fresh snow, and eyes that seemed to hold the gentle wisdom of the entire forest, starts his days with an effortless bounce. He hops along the mossy, leaf-strewn paths, offering his paws for a squirrel's overflowing basket of acorns, his ears for a hedgehog's tangled worries about the coming winter, or his keen nose to guide a young fawn back to its herd. In these early moments, the helping is pure magic, his chest swells with a warmth that feels like the sun's own embrace, his steps quick and joyful, the woods alive with the harmonious rustle of leaves and the distant call of streams. It's love in motion, a connection made tangible. But as the yeses accumulate, unexamined and unrelenting, the burds make their quiet entrance. One settles on his shoulder after a particularly long listening session, and another perches on his ear during an impromptu favor for a family of mice. They chirp softly at first, almost like cheerful companions sharing the trail. Barnaby, true to his nature, welcomes them; after all, isn't this what kindness looks like, making space for others' needs?

Yet, as the days blend into weeks, the carrying exacts its price, layer by subtle layer. What was once a springy hop slowed to a labored shuffle, each step pulling a little more from reserves he didn't know were finite. His fur, once gleaming with vitality, begins to lose its luster, matted slightly under the constant press of feathers and expectations. The forest, that vast, whispering sanctuary he cherished, starts to feel confining; the trees no longer arch welcomingly but loom as if adding to the weight, the paths narrowing under the weight of unspoken demands. Barnaby presses on, of course, his smile a fixed habit now, convincing himself that just a bit more effort, one more yes, will restore the lightness he remembers so fondly. He imagines the good feelings will return if he only tries harder and gives deeper. But the costs mount relentlessly: a tiredness that seeps into his bones, a quiet frustration that coils in his chest like a spring wound too tight, and a fading delight in the very woods that once fueled his spirit. It's only when the burds crowd so thickly, covering his back, his ears, even brushing his eyes, that he collapses to the forest floor, paws trembling, breath coming in short, ragged gasps, the path vanished beneath the flock. That moment of overwhelm isn't punishment; it's the forests and his own heart's way of saying, "See the cost. It's time to choose differently." And in the stillness that follows, with Sage's wise presence, the turning begins.

If Barnaby's arc feels like a mirror to your own experiences, you're not alone in that reflection; it's designed to hold space for exactly those moments. That gradual, almost imperceptible shift where what begins as a heartfelt gesture ends up demanding more than you have to spare. For the empaths among us, who can sense a room's unspoken tensions before they're voiced; for the caregivers who anticipate needs as naturally as breathing; for the people-pleasers who smooth every ripple to keep the waters calm, these costs land with particular familiarity. We offer our hands, our time, our listening because it's woven into the fabric of who we are, a beautiful thread of empathy and strength. But when boundaries remain unclaimed, the giving inverts: It becomes a drain rather than a delight, a weight rather than a wing. To bring this home without overwhelm, let's divide the primary costs into three digestible categories: the tiredness that lingers like morning mist, the quiet anger that simmers beneath the surface, and the lost joy that fades like twilight. For each, we'll use a short, actionable list to outline what it looks like in daily life, why it takes root, and a simple tip to spot it early. These are your trail markers, easy to scan, easy to apply, turning the vague sense of "something's off" into clear steps forward.

Cost 1: Tiredness That Sticks Around

This is the exhaustion that doesn't shake off with a good night's sleep or a strong cup of tea; it's the persistent drag that colors your hours, turning what should be ordinary into effortful.

- What it looks like in your day: Hitting snooze multiple times, not from a late night but from a bone-deep weariness; powering through a to-do list but with focus that wanders like a leaf in the wind; early evenings on the couch, scrolling aimlessly because even a book feels too heavy. Those small yeses, an extra errand for a neighbor, a late-evening check-in call, accumulate, making routines like meal prep or a quick walk feel like marathons.

- Why it takes root: The burds create a constant pressure on your energy reserves, leaving no true downtime for a refill. If fear of letting someone down or the habit of auto-yes skips the "wait, is this mine to carry?" moment, your tank depletes faster than it replenishes, especially in high-give roles like parenting or client-facing work.
- Spot it tip: At the end of your day, pause for one breath and ask: "Did I have even a small pocket of time just for me today?" If the answer is no or "barely," the burds are crowding your rest.

Jenna, a dedicated nurse in her mid-forties who balances demanding hospital shifts with being the reliable aunt for her sister's three energetic kids, experienced this cost in vivid detail. She said yes to every last-minute pickup from soccer practice, every shared recipe tweak over text, every "quick" family video call that stretched into hours. "I thought I was just being the dependable one, the rock," she reflected later in a coaching session. But by the time the family reunion rolled around, an event she helped plan from venue to playlist, she was a shadow of her usual self: Pale, with a persistent throb in her temples, barely tasting the home-cooked meal she'd contributed to. It wasn't a dramatic collapse or a sudden illness; it was the cumulative toll, the burds layering until her body whispered, "Enough," long before her mind could catch up. Her story is common among caregivers; the yeses feel noble at first, but they erode the very strength they aim to show.

Cost 2: Quiet Anger That Simmers Low

This isn't the thunderclap of a full-blown argument but the steady undercurrent of frustration, the slow boil that colors your inner dialogue and slips into your interactions without fanfare.

- What it looks like in your day: An involuntary eyeroll at a casual text like "Hey, can you grab that on your way?"; a sigh that lands heavier than intended when a coworker drops "one quick thing" on your already full plate; internal mutters of "Why is it always me?" during what should be a simple chat. It leaks out subtly, shorter replies to loved ones, a touch less patience for small hiccups, even irritation at neutral things like traffic after fulfilling a favor.

- Why it takes root: The imbalance of giving without receiving builds like pressure in a sealed jar, your efforts go unseen or unreciprocated, and resentment festers from the root belief that "they should know how much this costs me." Fear of confrontation keeps it bottled, turning kindness into a quiet grudge.
- Spot it tip: Tune into your body's first alert, a clench in your jaw, a twist in your gut, when an ask lands. That's the whisper: "This feels lopsided; time to notice."

Tom, a hands-on manager at a bustling local hardware store, lived with this simmering cost for months before it surfaced. He covered every shift gap for vacations or sick days, fixed broken displays long after closing, and trained new hires on what should have been his off-hours, all with a cheerful "Happy to help" that masked the growing knot inside. But beneath, the frustration coiled: "It's always landing on me, why doesn't anyone step up?" It began showing in small, telling ways: Gruffer tones in team group chats, less enthusiasm for the morning huddles that used to energize him, and one particularly tough evening where a misplaced inventory order sent him venting to his partner about "ungrateful" staff. "I didn't want to be the grumpy guy," Tom admitted during our work together. "But the anger was just building because no one saw the load I was shouldering alone." His burds weren't just tasks; they were symbols of an unseen sacrifice, turning his role from fulfilling to frustrating. Stories like Tom's highlight how quiet anger erodes from the inside out, making even the people we care about feel distant when the edge creeps in.

Cost 3: Lost Joy That Fades into the Background

This is the most poignant cost, the thief that steals in silence: the gradual dimming of what once brought genuine delight, crowded out by the constant call of needs.

- What it looks like in your day: Reaching for your phone to scroll instead of picking up that sketchbook or guitar that's been gathering dust; agreeing to a group outing but feeling "meh" amid the laughter, your mind elsewhere; a walk in nature where the birdsong registers but doesn't lift your spirit like it used to. The activities that used to hum with energy, a deep conversation, a creative project, a quiet hobby, now feel obligatory or out of reach.

- Why it takes root: The yeses fill every crevice of your time and heart, leaving no room for the "me-only" moments that recharge your soul. Habitual burds block the pause to ask "What fills me?" while the worth tie whispers that joy is selfish if it's not tied to helping.
- Spot it tip: At week's close, scan for one moment that should have sparked but didn't. If a yes stole the space, joy's waiting in the wings.

Sarah, the elementary school teacher who poured her passion into every classroom event, embodied this fading spark all too well. She said yes to organizing the fall craft fair, the winter reading night, and the spring field day relays, each with the belief that "the kids need this magic, and I can make it happen." But during a particularly packed term with a multi-week fundraiser layered on top, she stood in the school gym surrounded by balloons, cheering crowds, and the chaotic joy of children, and felt... nothing. "It was like I was directing a play about someone else's happiness," she shared, her voice catching. The delight in teaching, the way a student's "aha" moment used to light her up like fireworks, had dulled to routine. Her own joys? Postponed indefinitely: The weekends meant for tending her small balcony garden turned into supply runs; the evenings for curling up with a novel became grading marathons. Like Barnaby's forest losing its vibrant hum under the burds' constant chirp, Sarah's world had contracted to a series of duties, her inner light flickering low. Lost joy like this isn't always a loud alarm; it's the quiet absence, the "is this all?" that settles in when helping crowds out being.

These three costs don't operate in isolation; they interweave and amplify one another, creating a cycle that's hard to break without notice. Tiredness from unchecked yeses feeds the quiet anger ("I'm too drained to deal with this again"), which in turn blocks the pathways to joy ("Why bother trying when it all feels flat?"), and the resulting joy loss only deepens the exhaustion ("Nothing seems to refill me anymore"). For empaths, the emotional residue from others' stories adds an extra layer of weight, like burds that don't just perch but burrow in. Caregivers often feel it physically first, aches in the back from literal and figurative carrying, tension headaches from mental juggling. Professionals in helping fields, like therapists or managers, might notice it as a dip in their usual drive, where once-engaging work starts to feel like a grind rather than a calling. Barnaby's experience captured all three in one poignant collapse: His weary shuffle (tiredness), the unspoken frustration in his clipped helps (anger), and the way the woods' beauty blurred under the flock (lost joy).

To help you see these interconnections at a glance, without the overwhelm of dense paragraphs, here's a simple visual table. It's your pocket guide to the costs, with space to add your own notes. Print it, pin it, or jot in your journal; the goal is quick recognition, not perfection.

Cost Type	Key Signs (3-5 Daily Cues)	Linked Root (Ch. 1)	Early Spot Tip	Personal Note (Your Example)
Tired ness	Snooze marathon, foggy tasks, early crashes	Habit (auto-yes)	"Room to breathe today?"	
Quiet Anger	Eye-rolls, heavy sighs, "unfair" thoughts	Fear (let down)	Jaw clench on asks?	
Lost Joy	Scrolling over hobbies, “meh” in delights	Worth (give = matter)	Spark missing in fun?	

Fill the last column as you read, e.g., "Tiredness: Post carpool haze." It turns abstract into yours.

Why lift the lid on these costs right here, right now, in the midst of your full, demanding life? Because left unseen, they compound into a heavier flock than any single yes could create. The ripples extend far beyond the initial fatigue or frustration, touching every corner of your well-being. Start with health: That chronic tiredness isn't just inconvenient; it lowers your body's defenses, making you more prone to every passing cold or flu, slowing your recovery from minor bumps, and even influencing sleep patterns that leave you in a vicious loop of unrested days. The quiet anger, meanwhile, revs up your stress response like an engine idling too high; cortisol floods the system, tightening blood vessels, disrupting digestion, and inviting tension headaches or that constant knot in your shoulders. And lost joy? It's the silent partner to low mood, draining motivation to the point where even simple self-care feels pointless, creating a flatness that can edge toward deeper blues if not addressed. Basic research from burnout studies (the kind that's straightforward and relatable, not buried in jargon) shows that folks in helping roles with high, unchecked emotional loads report 30-40% more physical symptoms and mood dips than those who pause regularly. But the flip side is encouraging: Tools like the ones we're building here can cut that risk in half, fostering a resilience that lets you give from abundance, not scraps.

Relationships bear the brunt of these ripples, often in ways that feel the most painful because connection is what we give for in the first place. When carrying tilts lopsided, your yeses flow out while space for receiving stays narrow, distance creeps in uninvited. You start pulling back to protect what's left of your energy, sharing less of your true self because vulnerability feels too risky when you're already stretched thin. Loved ones sense the shift: "You're so busy lately," or "Everything okay?" they ask, not seeing the burds but feeling the coolness in your replies. Or the quiet anger leaks, turning a casual chat into a short one, a listening ear into a distracted nod, and trust frays at the edges. Tom's experience with his team is a textbook case: The constant covering led to resentment, which showed as less engagement in huddles, and soon the group dynamic felt tense rather than supportive. "They thought I was checked out," he said, "but I was just surviving." In family settings, it might mean holidays where you're the planner, but the joy's gone, or friendships that fade because you're always the listener, never the one heard. For Barnaby, his forest friends noticed the change; his help became rote, the warmth dimmed, and the woods adjusted awkwardly until his release allowed true flow again. The good news? Naming the cost early invites reciprocity; people step up when they see you're human, not a bottomless well.

Even your relationship with yourself takes a hit in these ripples, the quietest but perhaps deepest cost. Carrying burds blurs the lines of who you are beyond the helper role: "Am I just the fixer, the listener, the one who says yes?" Dreams and desires get sidelined, that book you meant to write, the trip you've daydreamed about, the quiet mornings with coffee and no agenda. The worth root amplifies it, whispering that joy for its own sake is indulgent if it's not tied to service. Lost joy reinforces the isolation, making self-connection feel distant, like reaching for a reflection in rippled water. But here's the empowering turn: Awareness, like the check-ins we'll explore, brings you back to center. Sarah's story shows it, she started small, reclaiming one evening for her garden, and watched her self-view sharpen: "I'm the teacher who creates, not just coordinates."

Different folks feel these ripples uniquely, so let's tailor a bit. If you're an empath, the emotional carry adds a fourth layer, absorbing others' energies like bonus burds that linger in your aura, amplifying tiredness and anger. Add a "mood residue" note to your spots. For caregivers, the physical toll hits hard, back strains from literal lifts, exhaustion from emotional holds, so body scans become key. Professionals or entrepreneurs? The drive dip can stall projects, turning momentum to mud; tie costs to goals: "Does this yes serve my bigger yes?" And in cultural contexts where "strong, silent giving" is prized, think family legacies of self-sacrifice, the guilt might whisper louder. Honor that heritage, but remember: Balance evolves it, making your care sustainable for generations.

With the costs laid out in those clear buckets, it's time to move from recognition to action, because seeing the weight is powerful, but tools make it liftable. Introducing the Check-In Questions: A set of five targeted, no-fuss prompts designed to scan your carrying regularly, much like a gentle patrol through your inner woods to note what's overgrown and what needs pruning. This isn't a rigid workbook exercise or a lengthy self-audit that adds to your load; it's a simple, flexible ritual to bring the costs into focus, helping you catch burds mid-landing rather than after they've nested. You'll need minimal setup, a quiet corner (kitchen table, car during lunch, bedside at night), and a place to capture thoughts: A dedicated notebook page, your phone's notes app, or even a voice memo if writing feels like one more task. Plan for ten to fifteen minutes once a week, Fridays are ideal, as the week's burds are still fresh in memory, but the weekend offers a soft landing for any insights. Over time, this practice becomes as natural as checking the weather before heading out: A quick forecast for your heart and energy, preventing storms before they gather.

Begin every check-in with a grounding ritual to create space; it's the Sage-like pause that lets truth surface without rush. Sit with your feet flat on the floor, imagining roots sinking into soft earth for stability. Place one hand on your heart or belly, the other open on your lap like a welcoming palm. Take three intentional breaths: Inhale slowly for a count of four, filling from the belly up to your chest (picture fresh air sweeping through the branches of your inner forest);

hold for four, noticing any tightness or flutter (no judgment, just witness); exhale for six, releasing whatever rises, like a burd lifting on a breeze. This mini sequence, less than a minute, resets your nervous system, shifting from reactive mode to awareness, just as Barnaby's stillness under the oak allowed the first burd to settle without alarm.

Now, dive into the five questions, answering in short bullets or phrases for ease, no essays needed. Keep it raw and real; this is for you, not a performance.

Energy Check: On a scale of 1-10, how full is my tank right now? What were the top one or two yeses that drained it most this week, and why did they pull so hard?

- Jot the number first, then the culprits: "4/10. Drained most by: Extra kid pickup (no time for my yoga); sister's vent call (emotional pull)."
- Why this question packs power: It pinpoints tiredness at its source, turning "I'm wiped" into "This specific yes took 3 points, time to adjust." Jenna, our nurse example, made this her anchor: Her tank often dipped to 3 after back-to-back family obligations. Tracking revealed the pattern,

"Aunt's unscheduled visits always cost 2 points, leading her to set a gentle 'Let's schedule for Thursday?' boundary. Within a month, her average climbed to 7, with more energy for the shifts she loved.

- Make it yours: If your tanks are under 5 more than twice a week, pair it with a proactive "recharge yes", something small like a 10-minute window for tea without interruptions or a playlist walk. Note how it shifts next time.

Heart Scan: Where's any resentment or quiet anger bubbling up today? Name the specific trigger and the 'why me?' thought underneath it.

- Example entry: "Bubbling at coworker's 'quick review' drop-in; thought: 'My lunch is always their buffer, feels unfair when I cover theirs too.'"
- Why it helps without harm: Naming the simmer diffuses it, like pointing a flashlight at a shadow, it shrinks. Tom's heart scan was a game-changer: "Trigger: Volunteered for weekend inventory again; why me? 'Proves I'm the reliable one, but no one offers back.'" Seeing it written freed him to suggest a rotation at the next team meeting, no

blowup, just balance restored, and his internal edge softened to occasional nudges rather than constant knots.

Make it yours: For empaths, add a sub-note: "Any mood residue from others sticking around?" Release with a whisper: "That's their feather now; mine lifts free." If anger shows three times weekly, flag for a deeper root dive (back to Chapter 1).

Joy Gauge: What brought even a small spark of delight this week, no matter how tiny? What burd or yes blocked more joy from flowing in?

- Example: "Spark: Shared a laugh over coffee with my dog (silly zoomies). Blocked: Late-night event prep stole my reading hour, left me flat."
- Why it rebuilds from the ground up: Focusing on sparks, even dim ones, trains your eye for light amid the load, while naming blocks reclaims space. Sarah's gauge transformed her weeks: "Spark: A kid's 'aha' during story time (that glow). Blocked: Fundraiser flyers till midnight, dimmed my garden time." She started batching prep into 30-minute sprints, freeing evenings; sparks multiplied, one rediscovered novel chapter led to

a full weekend of writing, joy edging back like dawn.

Make it yours: Rate the spark 1-10 for intensity. If averages under 4, brainstorm three "joy yeses" for the coming week: "Yes to a podcast commute," "Yes to calling that funny friend," "Yes to five minutes of stretching with music." Track how they nudge the needle.

Connection Pulse: For my top three relationships (partner, friend, colleague, self), what's the closeness level on 1-10? Where is the carrying creating a pull-back or distance?

- Example: "Partner: 5/10, warm but short talks; pull-back from always planning, no shared unwind. Friend: 7/10, good vents, but I'm the listener only."
- Why it mends the relational rifts: It highlights how costs strain bonds, inviting small bridges. Mike, the dad with endless fixes, used this to realign: "Kids: 6/10, fun bursts, but missed games from neighbor helps; pull-back: Too wiped for stories." He committed to one "no-fix" weekend; pulse

jumped to 8, with bedtime tales becoming ritual, closeness warming like a shared fire.

Make it yours: Include "self" as a fourth if solo seasons call. Low pulses? Note one "connect yes": "Share a real feeling tonight," "Text 'thinking of you' without advice."

Body Whisper: What signals is my body sending about the load today? Any tense spots, energy dips, or unexpected aches?

- Example: "Neck and shoulders knotted after back-to-back calls; dip in focus post-lunch from morning errands."
- Why it tunes you to the first alert: Bodies speak before words, Barnaby's trembling paws were the wake-up. Lisa's whispers were headaches from endless carpools: "Tight temples signal overstretch." Adding daily neck rolls and shared rides quieted them, body ease rising from 4 to 8. • Make it yours: Scan head-to-toe in 30 seconds. Rate overall 1-10. Low? Anchor with a "body yes": Warm shower, gentle shake-out, or hand on heart breath.

Close the check-in with a single, doable action: "This week, I'll lighten [one specific] by saying no to X and yes to Y." Keep it micro: "No to group chat pings after 8 p.m., yes to 10 minutes of journaling." Review at next session: "What shifted? Any wins, even tiny?" This loop turns insight to habit.

For an at-a-glance scaffold, here's an expandable table, copy to your notes or print for your wall. It's designed for quick fills, compartmentalizing without clutter.

Question	My Notes This Week (Signs/Triggers)	Action, I Took (Lighten Step)	Next Week's Shift (What Changed?)
Energy Check			
Heart Scan			
Joy Gauge			
Connection Pulse			
Body Whisper			

Jenna jazzed hers with colors: red for drains, green for sparks, yellow for actions, turning it into a playful dashboard. Her sister joined via shared notes; mutual check-ins doubled the encouragement, turning solo work into supportive sync.

What makes this tool so effective in the long game? It fragments the overwhelm, vague "I'm off" becomes "Energy at 4 from these two yeses", empowering small, immediate choices. Straightforward studies on emotional tracking (think accessible burnout lit) confirm weekly rituals like this slash fatigue by 25-30%, diffuse anger through articulation, and amplify joy by 20% via focused notice. It's your personal weather station for the inner forest: Spot a low-pressure system (anger brewing), adjust (one no), and watch clarity return.

The ripples of unaddressed costs deserve their own deep dive, as they touch far beyond the moment. Healthwise, tiredness acts like a lowered drawbridge, inviting every virus in, slowing wound healing, and even tilting hormones toward stress mode that affects sleep, appetite, and mood stability. Anger, that low simmer, floods you with cortisol like a constant alarm, constricting vessels (hello, tension headaches and tight chests), disrupting gut balance (bye, easy digestion), and weaving worry threads that snag on everything. Lost joy partners with a flattened effect, sapping the dopamine hits that fuel motivation, creating loops where "why try?" becomes default, edging toward persistent low energy or mild depressive shades. For helpers, the stats are stark but hopeful: One review of caregiving roles notes 35% higher symptom loads without check-ins, but consistent practices like this drop it by 40%, building a buffer of bodily bounce-back.

In relationships, the waves crash hardest because giving is your love language, yet an imbalance turns it sour. You become the default "yes machine," receiving sparse, leading to guarded hearts: Fewer deep shares (too risky when drained), shorter hangs (anger edges in), and a coolness that puzzles others. "What's wrong?" they probe, blind to burds but feeling the chill. Tom's team dynamic soured similarly, leans became loads, engagement dropped, trust thinned until he voiced it: "Lightning to stay present." Shares followed; bonds reknit stronger. Families see it in holidays gone tense (planner's resentment boils), friendships in one-way vents (listener burns out). But ripple reverse: Named costs invite equity, people step up, seeing your humanity, turning "go-to" to "go-together."

Self-ripples cut deepest, quiet as fog. Carrying erodes identity: "Am I more than the, yes?" Dreams defer, the course you eyed, the hobby paused, while worth lies: "Joy without give? Selfish." Joy loss amplifies isolation, self-view rippling, distorted. Yet check-ins mirror true: Sarah's gauges led to garden revivals, self-connection from "duty-doer" to "dream-weaver."

Tailor by you: Empaths, mood-residue line. Caregivers, physical deep-dive. Pros, goal-align: "Yes, fuel purpose?" Cultural givers, grace note: "Balance honors legacy." Guilt? Counter: "Whole me gives whole love." Barnaby's release? Wood's harmony, no's invited true yeses, care amplified.

Monthly, stack checks for trends: Tiredness fear-fed? Ch.1 revisit. Anger habitual? Pauses ahead. Joy worth-bound? Daily affirm: "My light rests too."

Share if it fits: "Check-in buddy, swap notes?" Jenna's duo sparked laughs, shared nos.

Costs are compassionate calls, not condemnations. See, scan, shift, you hop free. Barnaby rose; his forest sang.

Yours calls.

Chapter Reflection: Which cost tugs strongest, tiredness, anger, joy loss? Pick one question, try now. Note: What rose? One light step? Gentle, no ideals, just you.

CHAPTER 3:

WHAT IS A LOVING NO?

You've made it this far, friend, spotting those burds taking shape from old fears and habits, then facing the real ache of what happens when they stick around too long: the drag of tiredness, the low burn of anger, the way joy can slip off like dew in the morning sun. If any of that stirred something tender in you, that's good. It means you're listening, like Barnaby finally did when he sank to the forest floor, paws shaking under the flock. He didn't fight it right then; he just let the quiet come. And in that quiet, Sage showed up, not with fixes or lectures, but with a simple truth: "A no can be as kind as a yes." Those words hung there, soft as mist, shifting everything. They weren't a command or a cure-all. They were an invitation to see not as a wall, but as a way to breathe easier, to hop a little lighter.

That's what we're stepping into now: What a Loving No really means, not as some distant skill to chase, but as something you can touch today, a choice wrapped in care for yourself and the people around you. For so many of us who grew up smoothing edges and saying yes to keep the peace, the word "no" carries echoes from way back. It lands like a slammed door, sharp with rejection or the sting of someone pulling away. Maybe it was a teacher's firm "no" that felt like you weren't enough, or a friend's silence after you set a limit, leaving you to wonder if speaking up meant losing them. Those memories make you feel risky, like it might crack the connections we hold dear. But here's the warm truth your heart has probably whispered all along: No doesn't have to break anything. It can guard what's precious, your energy, your truth, the real love that flows when you're not stretched thin. A Loving No turns that old fear on its head. It's a boundary spoken from a clear place, not panic. It protects the ties that matter by keeping them honest, saying in a steady voice: "I choose truth here, with kindness for us both."

Let's name it plain, so it feels like a friend you can call on: A Loving No is your honest way of marking a limit, shared with respect for your own needs and the other person's heart. It sees what you can give right now, "My cup's low today", and gives a gentle nod to what they need, "I know this weighs on you." It's not turning your back on their ask or saying their feelings don't count.

It's owning that pushing past your edge doesn't serve anyone well. When you step into a Loving No, you're coming from a spot of knowing yourself, free from the scramble of guilt or endless "buts." Your words fall simple and calm, no big apologies trailing behind. And at the core? A quiet faith that truth like this strengthens bonds more than a half-hearted yes ever could.

You can feel it in the little moments. A coworker drops by with "Can you look at this report quickly?" and your gut tugs, a yes would add another burd, but no feels selfish. A Loving No steps in smoothly: "I hear how tight the deadline is, and I want to support. My afternoon's spoken for, but I can review first thing tomorrow, does that work?" It holds their worry without taking it on, claims your space without shutting the door. You're not pulling away; you're showing up clearer. That clarity? It's the gift. No resentment building later, no quiet pullback. Just room for the next yes to land true.

To help it all settle, let's walk through the two roads no can take, because not every no is the same, and knowing the difference can keep you on the kinder path. This isn't about right or wrong; it's about what energy you bring and what stays after. We'll lay it out side by side, simple as a fork in the trail, so you can see the way ahead.

The Reactive No: This is the one that bursts out when the tank's empty, after too many yeses have piled up without air. It's raw, often edged with the tiredness or anger from the last chapter, coming from a spot of pure survival. It might sound like: "No, I can't do it, I've got enough!" Or a quick "Not right now," with your voice tight, eyes flicking away. The push behind it? "Back off before I break." It gives a flash of relief, sure, one burd shakes loose. But then the aftertaste lingers: Guilt nips at you ("Did I hurt them?"), Or the air thickens with unspoken tension. The other person feels the shove, and you? You replay it, wondering if you "messed up" the connection. It's like gripping that fragile bird of a relationship too hard in fear; it bruises a little, even if it was to protect. Reactive Nos have their place as last stands, but they leave more mess than mending, guarding the fence, but letting the garden go wild.

The Loving No: This road opens up earlier, before the edge sharpens, pulled from the awareness you built in the last chapters, that pause to check your truth. You feel the ask come in, listen to your body's nudge (that sigh, that full-chest ease?), and name what fits without force. Words land gently: "This means a lot to you, and I care about that. My hands are full today, but let's find a time soon." The tone stays even, your gaze warm, breath steady. The feel underneath? Open but rooted, like a tree in the wind, bending without snapping. No shove, no scramble, just space: "I value us enough to keep this real." Like Barnaby's soft "I care, but not today," it lets the burd lift easily, no flap or fall. The bird? Wings get room, trust deepens. Loving Nos till the soil for healthier growth, less second-guessing after, and more steadiness in the bond.

Here's a quick table to hold the two side by side, jot your thoughts in the last column next time you're choosing.

Path	Trigger & Feel	Words/Tone Example	Aftermath for You & Them
Reactive No	Overload snaps; tight, pushy energy	"No, I'm done with this!" (sharp)	Quick ease, then guilt/tension
Loving No	Pause spots limit; calm, open energy	"I see your need; rest calls me now, tomorrow?" (steady)	Peace, connection holds

Glance at this when an ask lands, it's your reminder: Which path keeps the garden growing?

The energy in those words, that's where the shift lives deep. "No" on paper is just two letters, neutral as a blank branch. But breathed out? It carries your whole self, your day's weight, your heart's tilt. A Reactive No gusts out like a sudden wind, scattering to defend, but leaving branches bare. It tightens your shoulders, speeds your pulse, shouts "danger" to anyone nearby. A Loving No? It roots down, opens wide, grounded as earth after rain, flexible as grass in the breeze. Your stand eases: Shoulders soften, eyes hold kindness, voice flows even. No proof or plead; you simply stand true. That presence says safe: "This limit doesn't lock me; it makes us roomier." Barnaby knew it after his first chest loosened; the wood's song came back clear. No chaos, just calm.

Let's lean into a picture that fits our woods, to make the Loving No feel close as your next breath: Imagine cradling a small bird in your palms, the living pulse of a connection, all color and quick wing, but fragile if squeezed wrong. That's the tie with someone dear, full of promise but needing air to thrive. A Reactive No? It clamps in panic (fear crushes the flutter) or flings in frustration (startles it off course). A Loving No? Palms part slowly, fingers ease back tenderly, breeze flows, wings stretch free, the bird stays near but unbound. You're telling it, and them: "I hold our bond close enough not to smother it. I hold my own strength close enough not to let go. And I hold you close enough to let truth guide." Care like this never asks you to lose yourself. It knows a smothered yes clips both of you.

Why bring this up today, in the middle of your full plate? Because every no you swallow or yes you force through gritted teeth adds up like unpaid tabs, emotional debt that presses harder over time. More burds, steeper costs from the last chapter, until the load's a habit you can't shake. But every Loving No? It's settling the account with honesty, paying forward with the kind of integrity that frees you both. Look at the folks you lean on most, their yes and no both land solid, no games or guesswork. You trust their ground because it's steady, and it lets you stand easy on yours. When your no turns loving, you hand that trust back, a safe spot where they know your heart's open, even if the door's closed for now. Bonds like that? They deepen, not despite your limits, but because of them. At work, it means fewer rushed promises that flop, more space for the tasks that fit your gifts. With family, fewer bottled-up blowouts, more room for the laughs that last. For you? A growing faith in your own voice, the quiet win of "I showed up true."

In a world that cheers the endless yes, the hustle, the "lean in," the always-available heart, Loving Nos pulls you back to peace. They say boundaries aren't meant; they're the rich soil where your kindness takes deep root, grows tall without toppling. Barnaby's woods didn't fade after his nos; it greened up, the animals easing into asks that honored his whole self. Requests softened, his yeses glowed warmer. The forest felt alive again, full of real care. Your circle can shift the same, folks learn to meet you in the middle, your giving flows freer, joy sneaks back in.

Ready to feel it? Practice starts small, right where life offers an opening. Try this: Listening for the Loving No, a three-beat rhythm to tune your ear to truth, five minutes or less when an ask rolls in. No big prep; just you, pausing like Barnaby under the oak.

Pause and Tune In: The request hits, "Want to grab coffee?" or "Can you watch the kids tonight?", stop. One full breath: In slow, feel your feet root. Out easy, let the rush settle. Check your body, what's it saying? Lean in eager (green light)? Chest tight, shoulders up (yellow)? Pull back soft (that's the cue). No rush to decide; just notice, like watching a burd circle before landing.

Hear Your Quiet Truth: Push past the old voices, guilt's "They'll be mad," habit's "Sure, why not?", to the still spot underneath. Ask plain: "Do I have the time, heart, energy for this today?" If yes, lean into it fully. If no, name it kindly: "Rest feels bigger right now." This is your anchor, truth over tide.

Speak It Gentle: Soften first, smile if it fits, eyes warm, voice even. Lead with their side ("I get why these matters"), turn to yours ("My evenings for unwinding"), close with an open ("How about Thursday?"). Sample for a friend's vent: "That sounds rough, and I'm here for you. My head's full tonight. Can we unpack it over lunch tomorrow?" Clear words cut mix-ups; fuzzy ones invite more weight. Say it once, then let it land, no chase or fix.

Give it a go next chance you get, a low-stakes one, like passing on a group text add-on. After, note quickly: What eased in me? How'd they take it? Most times, it's softer than you think, a nod, "Got it, thanks," and the air clears. Do three this week; watch the habit form. If guilt tugs, remind yourself: "This is care, not cold."

Common bumps? "What if they push?" Hold steady, repeat your truth calmly: "I hear you; I still need this for me." "Will bonds break?" Real ones bend, not snap; they crave your full you. "Am I good at this yet?" Start tiny: No to solo menu choice, like "Pass on dessert, full thanks." Builds to bigger hops.

These nos ripple good too, they show balance is possible, inviting others to try. Work teams share fairer, families vent less bottled, you trust deeper: "My words work." Barnaby's first, no? One burd gone, woods wider, forest learned, his heart steadied.

This isn't the finish; it's the threshold. Reactive No: "You can't." Loving No: "Here's our way." Each one builds your trust inside, love no longer means losing yourself, limits no longer mean losing them.

Chapter Reflection: One question on the horizon? Pause: Body nudge? Truth call? Draft your line. Speak it, what softens? Note here. Wings grow one word at a time.

CHAPTER 4:

THREE PILLARS OF A LOVING NO

We've walked a good stretch together by now, uncovering how burds sneak in through those familiar roots of fear and habit, feeling the ache when they pile up too high, and then meeting the Loving No as that gentle doorway out. If Barnaby's story has woven into your thoughts like a thread through soft fur, that's no accident. Remember how he sat there after his collapse, the forest hushed around him, Sage's words landing like leaves in still water: "A no can be as kind as a yes." Barnaby didn't leap up, changed in a flash. He started small, testing that first honest "I care, but not today." One burd lifted, then another, as he learned to hold his truth without the old pull to fix or fill every gap. It wasn't magic; it was practice, built on a few steady pieces that held him up.

That's the heart of this chapter: The Three Pillars of a Loving No. Think of them as the sturdy legs under a table: clarity, compassion, and communication. They're not fancy or far-off; they're everyday strengths you already have, just waiting for a nudge to stand tall.

Together, they turn a shaky no into one that feels solid, kind, and true to you. We'll take each pillar slow, with a bit of why it matters, a simple tool to try, and a quick story from someone walking this path. No rush to master all three today, pick one that calls, like Barnaby choosing his first quiet stand. By the end, you'll have a map to lean on, one that makes Loving Nos feel less like a leap and more like a step you know by heart.

Let's start with the first pillar: **Clarity**. This is the foundation, the clear view of your own yes before any no, even whispers. Without it, we're guessing in the dark, saying yes to things that drain because we can't see what fills us, or no from fear without knowing our ground. Clarity isn't about listing every pro and con or having all answers lined up. It's the quiet knowing: What lights me up right now? What leaves me steady? Barnaby found his when he paused under that oak, the burds quiet for the first time. He saw his paws weren't made to carry everything; some loads were his to hold, others to let go. For you, it's the same; clarity spots your real yeses, so no's come from strength, not scrambling.

Why does this pillar matter first? Because a Loving No without clarity can wobble, rooted in guilt ("I should") or habit ("Always do"), it leaves you second-guessing after. But with it? No becomes a choice that honors your whole self. It frees energy for the yeses that matter, the ones where your heart hums true. In a week full of pulls, from work emails to family texts, clarity cuts the noise, letting you say no to the mismatch without the tug of "what if."

The tool here is straightforward: The Fill List. Grab a scrap of paper or your phone notes, five minutes, no perfection. Jot three things that fill you right now, big or small. Not "should" like "exercise" if it feels like a chore; real sparks, "A walk where my feet find the rhythm," "Brewing tea slow with no rush," "Losing time in a good book." Then, three things that drain, even if they're "good": "Late calls that steal my wind-down," "Planning everyone else's day." Look back: Patterns? Your yeses live in the fills; nos protect that space. Do this weekly, like checking the garden for weeds, to keep clarity fresh.

Take Elena, a social worker who came to coaching with burds thick as Barnaby's flock. She said yes to every client overlap, every team brainstorm, until her evenings blurred into exhaustion. "I thought helping was my fill," she said. But her list showed different: Fills, "Quiet mornings with my journal," "Baking bread just for the smell," "Calls with my sister where we laugh out loud." Drains, "Back-to-back meetings that leave no air," "Taking home others' stories without shake-off." Clarity hit: Her real yes was present, not present everywhere. She started no's like "This week's full; let's book for next Tuesday." One burd gone, then two, energy returned, her work sharper, joy in baking warmer. Quick win: Elena's list became her phone wallpaper, a glance before yeses. Nos flowed more easily, guilt faded.

Clarity builds the base, now, the second pillar: **Compassion.** This one's the soft hold, the open heart that wraps around your no without letting old shame sneak in. It's not fluffy self-talk or ignoring limits; it's the kindness you give freely to others, turned inward. "You're doing enough," it says, or "This choice honors your care." Barnaby touched it when Sage sat beside him, no fixing, just presence: "You've carried so much." That compassion didn't judge his load; it saw the courage in it, then the grace in release. For us, it's the voice that quiets "You're selfish" to "You're human, and that's okay."

This pillar matters because no's without compassion can feel cold, even to you. Guilt rushes in, whispering "Bad friend, bad teammate," turning a healthy limit into a wound. But with compassion? No lands warm, like a hand on a shoulder. It keeps your heart open, so connections stay tender, not tense. In the pull of daily asks, compassion says, "I choose me here, and that's love too."

The tool is a Kindness Anchor, a short phrase you whisper or write before a no, like a talisman. Craft one that fits: "My no makes room for truer yes," or "I care by caring for me first." Say it in the pause, after clarity spots the limit, before words go out. Pair with a breath: Hand on heart, feel the beat, let the phrase sink. Use it daily, even on small no's like "No seconds, thanks, full and grateful."

Meet Rachel, a mom and part-time counselor whose days run on yes, school runs, client calls, and meal trains for neighbors. Burds piled until anger simmered low. Her anchor? "Kindness starts at home." Before a no to a last-minute "Can you host?" she breathed it in:

Clarity said her evening needed quiet; compassion added, "This isn't mean, it's mercy." Words out: "I love our hangs, but tonight's for recharge. Coffee Friday?" The friend nodded, "You deserve that." Rachel felt the shift, no guilt bite, just ease. Quick win: Her anchor stuck on the fridge; no's to kid extras ("Not tonight, let's read instead") built family calm, her patience fuller. Compassion turned limits into gifts.

These pillars link, clarity names the need, compassion holds it kindly. Last, **Communication:** The clear voice that shares your no without blur or bite. It's the words that land honestly, calmly, leaving room for understanding. Not stiff memorized script, but your tone steady, eyes warm, message simple: Their ask seen, your truth said, door ajar if it fits. Barnaby's "I care, but not today" was pure this, short, true, heart open. No ramble, no wall.

Communication matters because no's unspoken fester, spoken sharp sting. But clear? It builds trust, "I know where she stands, and it's safe." In tangled spots, work demands, family pulls, it cuts confusion, invites "Okay, how else?"

Tool: The No Bridge, three-part flow for words: Acknowledge ("I see this for you"), State ("My space is..."), Offer ("Let's try..."). Customize: Home, "Love our chats; evenings recharge me now, morning walk?" Work, "Tight deadline, I get it; my load's full, team handoff?" Friends, "That trip sounds fun; budget's tight, local hike soon?"

David, a teacher dad, used this for parent emails piling up. Clarity: "After-hours drain." Compassion: "This serves us better." Bridge: "Your concern's clear; grading's my evening, reply by noon tomorrow?" Responses warmed, "Thanks for the time." Quick win: David's bridge email template cut late-night worry, sleep deepened, mornings brighter.

Pillars together? Clarity spots, compassion holds, communication shares, like Barnaby's slow rise, flock thinning, hop returning.

To tie the pillars quickly, here's a table, your practice map, with space to note your first tries.

These pillars aren't just ideas—they're tools you can hold and try. To help them stick, here's a simple table you can copy into your notebook or phone. It gives you a quick snapshot of each pillar, its feel, the tool that brings it to life, and a real-life quick win from someone who's walked this path. Seeing it laid out like this makes the pillars feel less like concepts and more like friends you can call on.

First, here's an **example** filled in with stories we've already met, so you can see how it looks when someone actually uses it:

Pillar	Core Feel & Why It Holds	Tool Snapshot	Quick Win Example
Clarity	Know your yes to own your no	Fill List: 3 fills, 3 drains	Elena's journal mornings freed
Compassion	Kind heart to self in the choice	Anchor Phrase: "No makes truer yes"	Rachel's "kindness home" eased guilt
Communication	Clear words that keep doors ajar	No Bridge: Acknowledge, State, Offer	David's email boundaries-built trust

Look how each pillar connects to a real person's life—Elena, Rachel, David. It shows the tool in action and the small shift that followed. You don't need to fill every box perfectly; the point is to see that these pillars are practical, not perfect.

Now here's a **blank version** for you to use. Copy it down, or take a photo of this page. Fill it in as you experiment with one pillar this week—maybe start with the one that feels closest to your heart right now.

Pillar	Core Feel & Why It Holds	Tool Snapshot	Quick Win Example	Your Test Note
Clarity				
Compassion				
Communication				

Glance here before asking, pick one pillar to lead. Over time, they weave seamlessly, feeling like natural breath.

Examples show it in motion. Quick wins: Clarity for Sarah, list cut event yeses, joy sparked in paints. Compassion for Tom, anchor "You matter resting" softened team no’s, resentment lifted. Communication for Jenna, bridge to family, "I see the need; shift's long, weekend call?" eased pull-backs, bonds warmed.

These pillars aren't solo; they lean on each other. Clarity without compassion? Nos feel bare. Compassion without words? Limits stay silent. Communication without ground? They waver. Barnaby's no’s worked because all three hummed truths, seen, heart kind, voice steady. His wood bloomed: Animals asked wiser, yeses landed full. Yours can work flows fairer, family feels seen, and you stand taller.

Bumps come, guilt tugs ("Too soft?"), push-back ("But I need..."). Meet with pillars: Clarity ("My truth holds"), compassion ("This is care"), communication ("Let's find a fit"). Start small, one pillar a week. Clarity first if fog's thick; compassion if shame nips; communication if words stick.

This builds the how for next, practice steps, and scripts. Pillars are your stand; now, the walk.

Chapter Reflection: Which pillar pulls you, clarity, compassion, or communication? Pick one, try the tool today. What shifts? Jot down: Feels? Next step? One at a time, like burds lifting slowly.

CHAPTER 5:

HOW TO PRACTICE THE LOVING NO

We've built a good foundation together, haven't we? From spotting those burds as they first flutter in, tied to our old fears and habits, to feeling the slow ache of what happens when they nest too long, the tiredness that clings, the anger that simmers quietly, the joy that fades like fog lifting off the lake. Then we met the Loving No itself, that kind doorway out, and the last chapter gave us the three pillars to hold it steady: clarity to know your ground, compassion to wrap it gently, and communication to share it truly. If Barnaby were here, hopping along beside us, he'd nod slowly, his ears twitching with that rabbit wisdom. Remember how he didn't change in a rush after Sage's words? No grand speech or instant flight. He practiced, one small no at a time, "I care, but not today," his voice soft as moss underfoot. Each one lifted a burd, light as a leaf turning in the breeze, until his paws felt the earth again, his fur caught the sun's full shine. That's the beauty of practice: It turns knowing into doing, one breath, one word at a time.

This chapter's where we roll up our sleeves, not for heavy work, but for the steady rhythm of trying. How do you weave a Loving No into the weave of your days, with all their pulls and pings? We'll walk it step by step, like following a path through the woods: Pause to listen, check in with your truth, speak it clearly. Then, real-life scripts for the spots where it counts, family tugs, work extras, and friend vents that go long. And because guilt can tag along like an old shadow, we'll add release tools: Simple breaths to settle, journal pages to dump the what-ifs. No pressure to get it perfect; this is for the mornings when the ask lands before coffee, the evenings when your tank's low. By the end, you'll have a handful of ways to try, like seeds to plant where they fit. Barnaby didn't clear his flock overnight. He hopped, paused, tried again. You can too, small steps that add up to an open sky.

Let's start with the flow itself, the three-beat heart of any Loving No. It's not a formula carved in stone, but a natural rhythm, like the in-out of breath when you're walking easily. Draw from the pillars we know: Clarity names your limit, compassion holds it kindly, and communication lets it land. But in the moment, it boils down to this: Pause, check in, speak your truth. Simple as that, but oh, the space it opens.

First, the pause, that holy breath before the yes or no tumbles out. Life doesn't always give warning; requests come in texts that buzz mid-meal, emails that pop up during your one quiet minute, or voices at the door when you're halfway through your own day. The pause is your anchor, the moment you claim to listen inward. It's one full breath, or two if you can, feet on the ground, hand on your belly if it helps, feel the rise and fall. No big meditation; just stop the autopilot. Why pause? Because without it, we're back to reactive no or drained yes, burds landing before we see them. Barnaby's pause came under the oak, the flock still, but his heart finally heard. Yours might be in the kitchen, phone in hand, feeling the tug. Pause, and the world slows just enough to choose.

From there, check in, turn that pause into a quiet ask of yourself. What's true here? Use clarity: "Does this fit my tank today, energy, time, heart?" Compassion adds: "What do I need to show up kind for them?" It's a 10second scan: Gut twist for no, chest open for yes. If it's a no, name it soft, no story needed yet, just "Rest calls louder," or "My hands are full." This check pulls from your Fill List in Chapter 4. Does it fill or drain? Jenna, the nurse we met, made this her habit: A family call comes, "Can you run by the store?", pause, check: "Tank at 4, drain if I go." Truth: "Not tonight." The pause saved her evenings, one breath at a time.

Last in the flow, speak your truth, the communication that brings it out into the light. Keep it short, warm, like Barnaby's purr: Acknowledge their ask ("I see these matters"), state your limit ("My evenings for rest"), offer a bridge if it fits ("Tomorrow morning?"). Tone matters more than polish, eyes soft if in person, words steady in text. No long explanation; that's a habit trick. The goal? Clear enough to honor, kind enough to hold. David, the teacher dad, practiced this for parent queries: "Deadline tight, I get it; grading's my night, reply by lunch?" Parents eased, "Thanks for the heads-up." Speaking truth turned overload to order, his sleep steadier.

This flow isn't linear always, pause might blend with check, speak with a quick compassion whisper. Try it on small stakes first: No to an extra cookie, yes to the song on the radio. Build the muscle, and bigger asks feel less like cliffs. Why this rhythm? It turns from fight to flow, burds lifting not in storm but breeze. Barnaby's practice? Forest adjusted, friends asked less, listened more. Your days can shift the same: Work eases, home warms, you breathe deeper.

Now, let's make it real with scripts, words you can borrow or bend for the spots where burds love to land. These aren't rules; they're starters, pulled from the No Bridge, tailored for family, work, friends. Use the flow: Pause-check-speak, pillars underneath. Start with family, where asks come wrapped in love but land heavily.

Family Scripts: These tugs hit close: "Mom, can you watch the kids?" or "Sis, help plan the trip?" Pause for the old pull to please, check your truth (tank low after your day?), speak with the bridge that keeps ties tender.

- "I love being there for you, and I see how this eases your week. My evenings are for my own unwind, how about Saturday morning?" (For the last-minute kids.)
- "This trip planning sounds fun, and I'm in for the memories. Budget's tight for me right now, let's focus on local spots first?" (For the big ask that stretches.)

- "Your story matters, and I'm listening. My head's full from work, can we pick it up over coffee tomorrow?" (For the vent that goes long.)

Rachel, the mom-counselor, used the first for her sister's "emergency" dinners: Pause (tired from clients), check ("Need my bath"), speak the script. Sister: "Okay, thanks for saying." Dinners became chosen, not chained; Rachel's patience grew, and her family felt her fuller.

Work Scripts: Boss extras or team "favors" pile quick, "Cover this meeting?" or "Review my draft?" Pause before the habit, yes, check (does it fit your load?), speak to keep doors open without overload.

- "I appreciate the trust in me for this, and I want the team to be strong. My plate's full with [project]; can we loop in [colleague] too?" (For the shift cover.)
- "This draft's important, I see that. Deadline's tight for me, feedback by the end of the day Monday?"

  (For the quick review.)

- "Meeting sounds key, and I'm for the goals. Afternoon's blocked for [task], morning slot work?" (For the overlap.)

Tom, the shop manager, leaned on the second for inventory asks: Pause (weekend family time), check ("Drains my recharge"), speak. Boss: "Fair, thanks." Team shared more, Tom's energy steady, work felt partner, not pull.

Friend Scripts: Vents or hangs that drain, "Let's meet now?" or "Tell me everything." Pause for the empathy tug, check (your day's arc?), speak to keep the bond without burnout.

- "I'm glad you reached out. This weighs heavily, I hear. My night's quiet time; lunch tomorrow to dive in?" (For the sudden vent.)
- "That outing calls fun, and I miss our laughs. Schedule's packed, coffee catch-up next week?" (For the spontaneous plan.)
- "You win big, and I'm cheering. Energy's low after [day]; call soon to celebrate properly?" (For the share that needs space.)

Elena, the social worker, tried the first for a friend's crisis text: Pause (post-session empty), check ("Need Walk alone"), speak. Friend: "Take your time, here when ready." Walks became ritual, friendship deeper, true listens, not tired ones.

These scripts bend, swap words to your voice, and add compassion's "I care" if it fits. Practice aloud, mirror or air, to feel the flow. Once a day, and nos land is natural.

Guilt tags along sometimes, that old shadow whispering "You should've." Release it with tools, breath for quick settling, and a journal for a deeper dump. Breath first: The Burd Release, sit, hand on heart, breathe in "I choose kind," breathe out "Guilt lifts like a feather." Three rounds, feel the ease. Journal: "Guilt page", dump the what-ifs ("They'll think I'm cold"), then flip: "Truth: This no lets me give better." Burn or close the page; let it go. Lisa used breath after carpool no's: In-out three, shadow faded. Journal weekly turned guilt into growth.

Practice like this? Burds thin, days open. Barnaby's hops returned, forest sang. Yours will too.

Let's linger on the why of practice, because it's the soil where these steps take root. Why bother with pauses and scripts when yes feels easier, safer? Because unpracticed nos stay stuck, reactive bursts that leave you ragged, or swallowed yeses that build resentment slowly. But this flow? It turns into rhythm, a hop you trust. Clarity in the check keeps you true, compassion in the breath keeps you tender, communication in the bridge keeps you connected. Over time, it rewires: Asks land less heavy, your voice stronger, guilt a visitor, not a resident. David's work no’s? From dread to done, the team trusted his word, his home time sacred. Practice isn't perfection; it's presence, one tries to build the next.

For deeper release when guilt clings, layer in the tools. Breath's your fast friend, try the 4-7-8 for stuck moments: In 4 (fill belly), hold 7 (feel hold), out 8 (let shadow go). Whisper "This is not love" on the out. Jenna breathed it post-family script: Guilt tugged ("Selfish aunt?"), Release whispered no, sleep came easily, mornings clear. Journal's your longer listen: "Dump page", free-write the fear ("They'll pull away"), then "Truth page" "This no invites real us." Date it, fold it away. Weekly review: Patterns? Wins? Elena's dumps turned to celebrations: "Three nos, three frees." Tools like these empty the cup for clearer flow.

Real spots call for tweaks, family's emotional, work's professional, friends' casual. Family: Lean compassion heavy, bridge wide, "Love you, this is my now." Work:

Clarity sharp, offer concrete, "Monday." Friends: Tone light, acknowledge warm, "Your heart's big, mine needs quiet." If push-back comes ("But I really need..."), pause again: "I hear that; still true for me." No defense; just hold. Tom's push-back? Boss: "But you're good at it. "Tom: "Appreciate; still full." The boss shifted, load shared.

Examples light the way. Quick win for Lisa: Family script after carpools, "Love helping, but shifts long, alternate weeks?" Mom: "Fair, your turn off." Carpools are fairer, and Lisa's headaches are gone. For work, Rachel's bridge to extra session: "Client's key, I see; my week's packed, co-lead?" Colleague stepped up, Rachel's boundaries held, clients felt her full. Friend vent for Sarah: "Rough day, I get it; mine's wind-down." Friend: "Yes, rest well." Vent became chat, and friendship eased.

Practice weekly: One flow try, one script test, one release. Track in a note: Ask | Flow Step | What Landed | Shift Felt. Do patterns show more easily with texts? Harder face-to-face? Adjust gently. Barnaby practiced in the woods' hush, first nos wobbly, then sure. Forest met him there, asks truer. Your world waits the same, pulls soften, yeses shine.

Bumps? "Forgot to pause." Kind: "Next breath." "Guilt stayed." Release again. "They took it wrong." Check your part, hold theirs. Practice builds forgiveness, too, for you first.

This flow, scripts, releases, they're your toolkit, light as a pouch on the trail. Nos become notes in a song, not stumbles. Burds fly freer, your hop returns.

Chapter Reflection: Try one script this week, what spot calls? Pause-check-speak it. What shifts, ease, guilt, bond? Jot here. Small tries, big skies.

CHAPTER 6:

FREEDOM & FLOW: RELEARNING THE LOVING YES

Here we are, at the wide-open end of our path together, the place where the trees thin out and the sky stretches full above, like the moment Barnaby finally shook off the last burd, his paws touching earth light as a sigh. Remember that scene?

The forest had gone still after his collapse, the flock heavy and humming, but as he practiced those first quiet no's, "I care, but not today", "one burd after another", caught the breeze and lifted free. It wasn't dramatic; no rush of wind or sudden soar. Just space, breath by breath, until his hop came back bouncy, his fur caught the sun's glow again, and the woods felt like home, not a weight to bear.

The animals noticed too, their asks softened, their company warmer, because Barnaby showed up whole. His yeses? They landed differently now, not pulled from empty, but chosen from full. That's the gift waiting here, in this final stretch: Freedom and flow, where no makes room for a yes that feels like singing, not striving.

If you've walked with me this far, spotting burds in their sneaky starts, naming the tiredness and quiet anger they bring, learning the Loving No with its pillars of clarity, compassion, and clear words, then practicing that pause-check-speak Rhythm in the thick of family pulls, work extras, friend vents, you might already feel a shift. Breathe easier in the mornings, a no that lands without the old tug of guilt, a yes that lights you up because it's yours first. But if some spots still feel wobbly, that's okay too. This isn't a race to perfect; it's a trail to wander, one hop at a time. And now, as we turn toward home, let's linger on what blooms after the release: Relearning the Loving Yes. Not the old yes, the one that gathered burds like habits we couldn't shake. This is the yes that flows from freedom, the one where giving feels like a gift you wrap for yourself first, then share with hands steady and heart open.

Picture Barnaby after his practice took hold. The woods weren't silent anymore; They hummed with a new rhythm. A squirrel scampered up with a nut basket too heavy for her paws, "Barnaby, a hop?", and he paused, true as ever, checking his morning light. Yes, came easily: "Let's go," and they bounced along the path together, his ears perked, her chatter light. No flock followed, no drain after. That yes filled him, the way a clear stream fills a cup, overflowing just enough to offer a sip without spilling himself dry. The forest thrived on it: Animals came not from need alone, but from the pull of his full presence. His listening went deeper, his helps quicker, his laughs rang farther. Joy returned not as a flash, but as the steady shine in his fur, the easy curve of his hop. It's the same promise for you:

When no's clear the clutter, yeses land chosen, and balance blooms. Giving stops being a grab for worth or a shield from fear; it becomes the natural outpour of a heart that's rested, rooted, and ready.

Why does this matter as our wrap? Because the Loving No isn't the end, it's the clearing for what comes next. We've spent time on the hard part, the letting go, but freedom's the fruit: A life where help feels good again, connections run deep without drain, and your days hold more you. That tiredness from Chapter 2? It lifts when yeses fit your flow. The anger? It quiets when giving from full, not force. Joy? It sticks around, sparked by choices that honor your whole self.

Barnaby didn't become less kind after his nos; he became more himself, his yeses warmer, the woods richer for it. You, with your empath's ear or caregiver's hands, deserve that same return: Help that hums, bonds that breathe easy, a quiet inside that says "enough" without emptiness.

This relearning isn't magic or a sudden switch. It's the slow unfurl, like watching a fern open to the sun after rain. No clears the weeds, those obligation yeses that left you bent. Now, space opens for the ones that root deep: The yes to a walk alone that clears your head for better listening later. The yes to a friend's story because your cup's brimming, not borrowed. The yes to your own small dreams, a class you've eyed, a trip with no strings, because you've made room. Balance builds here: Nos as the roots that hold you steady, yeses as the branches reaching out. Joy sneaks back in the gaps, the laugh that comes unbidden, the rest that restores, the help that feels like play. It's the flow Barnaby found: Give when it fits, rest when it calls, love without losing your light.

Let's lean into how this looks in the everyday, because that's where the relearning lives. Start with the shift in your help, they become chosen, not chased. That coworker drop-in? Before, yes, from habit, burd after. Now, pause: "My afternoons for this report, tomorrow?" If yes fits later, it lands full; your input is sharp. Family dinner? No to the full spread if your week's long, yes to the pie you love baking. The table feels warmer; your stories flow freer. Friends' vent? Yes, when your ears are open, no when they're not, the share goes deeper, trust thicker. Work project? Yes, to the piece that sparks you, no to the stretch that doesn't, your best shines, team benefits. It's not less giving; it's giving that gives back, joy woven in because it's yours.

Elena, the social worker with her flock of client overlaps, felt this bloom after her no’s took hold. Her first practices were shaky, scripts for team meets, anchors for guilt, but as burds lifted, yeses changed. A client calls? Yes, to the one that tugged her heart, no to the rushed addon. Her presence deepened, and breakthroughs came easier. Evenings? Yes, to her journal, the pages filled with sparks she'd forgotten. "It's like the woods opened," she said. "Helping feels like me again, not a mask." Her balance? Weekends for sister laughs, not catch-up work, joy stuck, resentment gone.

To make this relearning yours, let's add a tool: The Weekly Yes Map. It's a simple sketch to celebrate the chosen yeses, turning "what I did" to "what filled me."

Sunday evenings work best,10 minutes, paper or phone. Draw a circle for your week, divide into days or spots (work, home, self). Mark your yeses with stars:

Big ones like "Yes to the team brainstorm, sparked ideas," small like "Yes to tea break, breathed easy." Nos get gentle dots: "No to extra shift, room for walk."

Look back: What patterns light the map? Fills clustered in mornings? Drains from evenings? Adjust next week, one more yes to what hums, one no to what pulls. No judgment; just notice, like Barnaby watching his hop return.

Tom, the shop manager, mapped his first: Stars on "Yes to staff lunch, laughed real," dots on "No to late fix, home dinner hot." Patterns? Yeses filled when shared, not solo. Next week, he yessed a team game, bonds warmed, his shine back. Map became fridge art, weeks flowing freer.

Rachel's map showed family yeses draining, dots on no's to full plans, stars on "Yes, to park with kids, easy joy." She shifted: Yes, to short hangs, no to marathons. Balance bloomed, mornings hers, evenings theirs, heart full without fray.

This map isn't a tally; it's a mirror, showing how no opens yeses that stick. Joy returns chosen: The hobby, yes, because space allows, the help, yes, because energy flows. Balance feels like a river, give and receive in turn, no dams or floods. Connections deepen: People meet your full self, ask truer, thanks warmer.

Barnaby's yeses? Forest sang, squirrel's basket shared, hedgehog's worry lightened, all from his steadiness.

What if old burds tug? Guilt whispers "Less yes, less you"? Pause, pillar up:

Clarity ("This yes fits now"), compassion ("You're kind resting"), map it out ("Last week's stars prove"). Practice holds, weeks turn to habit, flow to freedom.

As we close this chapter, hold this: You've cleared ground for yeses that honor your light. Barnaby hopped free, whole.

Chapter Reflection: What's one yes calling you now, small hop, big branch?

Map it: Where does it fit? What makes room? Jot here. Say it aloud, feel the flow begin.

Thank you for letting this book be a guide in your journey.

If it helped you, a review would mean the world to me.

To continue your journey with more resources, reflections and community: visit www.sparklingessence.com

With gratitude,

Laura

www.ingramcontent.com/pod-product-compliance
Lightning Source LLC
LaVergne TN
LVHW090535110826
845146LV00003B/1106